PRIMATES

LEMURS

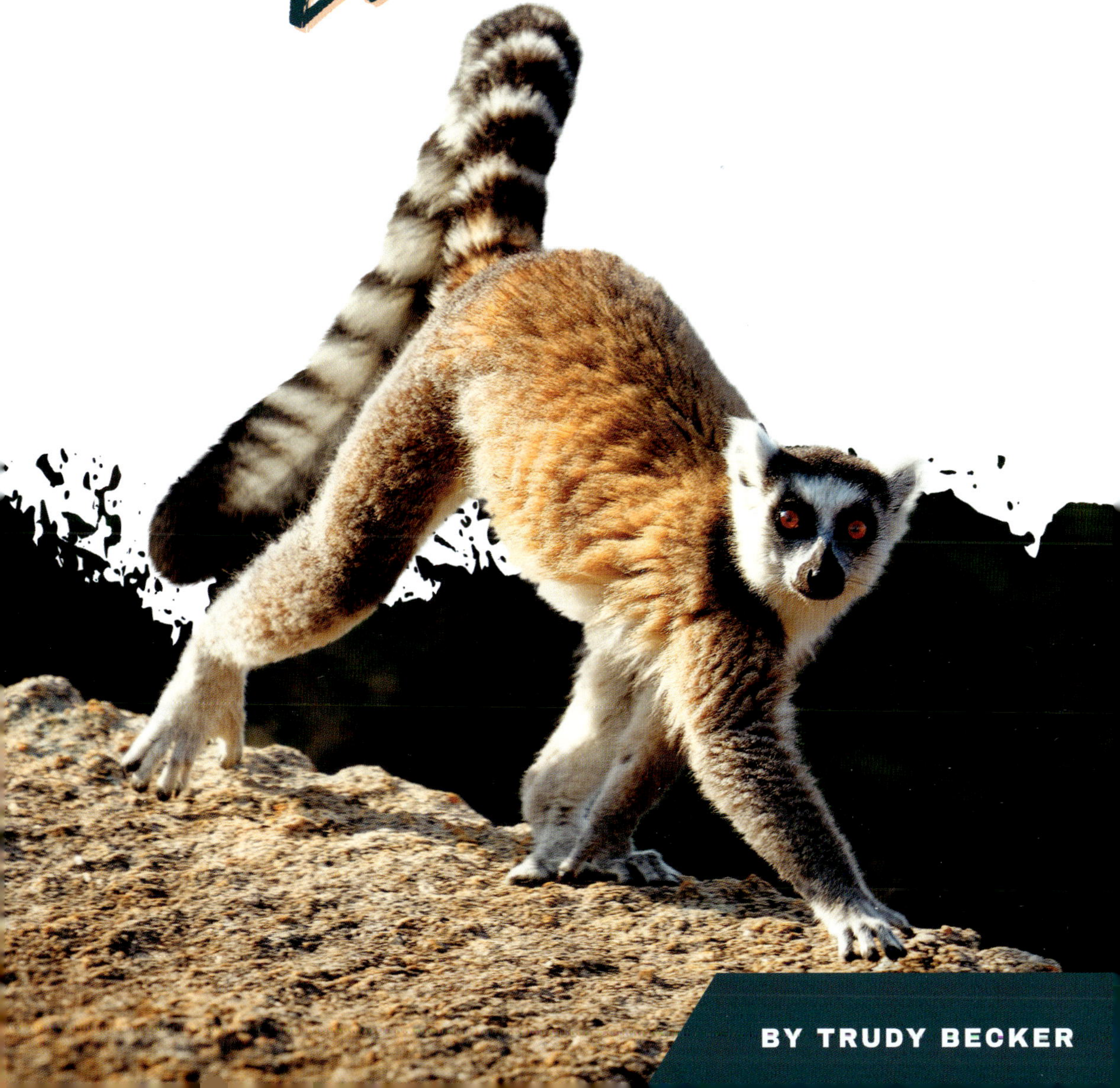

BY TRUDY BECKER

WWW.APEXEDITIONS.COM

Apex is distributed by North Star Editions:
sales@northstareditions.com | 888-417-0195

Produced for Apex by Red Line Editorial.

Photographs ©: Shutterstock Images, cover, 1, 4–5, 6, 7, 10–11, 13, 14, 18–19, 20–21, 21, 24, 26, 29; iStockphoto, 8–9, 12, 15, 22–23; Cal Holman/500px/Getty Images, 16–17; Moment Open/Getty Images, 25

Library of Congress Control Number: 2025939145

ISBN
979-8-89250-796-7 (hardcover)
979-8-89250-825-4 (paperback)
979-8-89250-881-0 (ebook pdf)
979-8-89250-854-4 (hosted ebook)

Printed in the United States of America
Mankato, MN
012026

NOTE TO PARENTS AND EDUCATORS

Apex books are designed to build literacy skills in striving readers. Exciting, high-interest content attracts and holds readers' attention. The text is carefully leveled to allow students to achieve success quickly. Additional features, such as bolded glossary words for difficult terms, help build comprehension.

TABLE OF CONTENTS

Three lemurs sit in a tall tree. They munch on leaves and flowers. One lemur watches for danger.

Lemurs may help one another find food.

A fossa crouches on a lower branch. It is about to attack. But one lemur sees it. The lemur lets out a loud shriek. The other lemurs hear it and start to run.

A fossa is a cat-like animal that hunts and eats lemurs.

Some lemur calls can be heard more than 1.2 miles (2 km) away.

TALKING TOGETHER

Lemurs make many noises. They bark, grunt, and yell. Some noises are warnings. Lemurs may alert one another of danger. Or they may tell other lemurs to stay out of their **territory**.

Sifakas are a type of lemur. They can leap 40 feet (12 m) between trees.

The fossa chases them. But the lemurs are too fast for it. They leap quickly from tree to tree.

FAST FACT

Lemurs have pads on their hands and feet. The pads help them stick to trees.

CHAPTER 2

ALL ABOUT LEMURS

Lemurs are **primates**. There are more than 100 lemur **species**. They come in different colors and sizes. Most have big eyes and long tails.

A ring-tailed lemur's tail can be 2 feet (0.6 m) long.

Indri lemurs are the largest type of lemur. They can weigh up to 21 pounds (10 kg).

The biggest lemurs grow about 28 inches (71 cm) long. The smallest are less than 5 inches (12.7 cm) long.

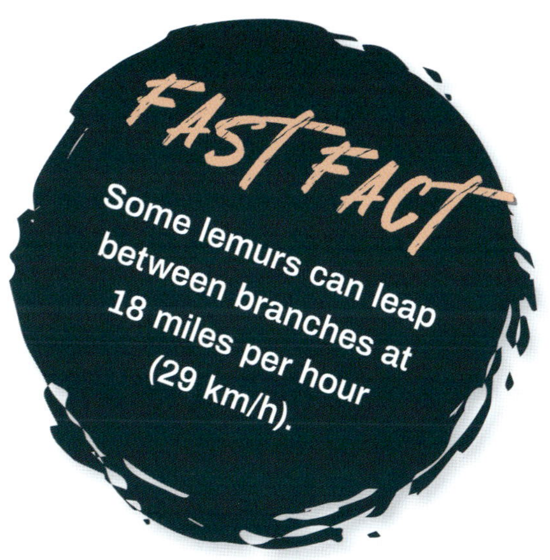

The Madame Berthe's mouse lemur is the smallest kind of lemur. It could fit in a teacup.

Mongoose lemurs are one of the few types found outside Madagascar. Some live on the nearby Comoro Islands.

Lemurs live only in Madagascar and nearby areas. They can have several types of **habitats**. Many lemurs live in rainforests. Others live in dry or rocky areas.

WETLAND LEMUR

The Alaotra reed lemur lives near Lake Alaotra. That is Madagascar's biggest lake. The lemur lives in plants that grow by the water.

The Alaotra reed lemur lives in one small area. Its habitat range is only 49,000 acres (20,000 ha).

CHAPTER 3

LIFE IN THE WILD

Different lemur species have different diets. Some lemurs mainly eat plants. Others also eat insects, tree sap, or even birds.

An aye-aye is a type of lemur with long, thin fingers. It can dig insects out of trees.

A lemur's big eyes help it see in the dark.

Some lemur species look for food during the day. But most species are nocturnal. They are active at night.

FAST FACT

Lemurs have strong noses. They can smell fruit from 50 feet (15 m) away.

Many lemurs spend most of their lives up in trees. Some types do go down to the ground. But they stay close to tree trunks. They can climb quickly if danger comes.

Ring-tailed lemurs spend more time on the ground than most other species.

Humans in Madagascar often cut down trees for farming.

LOSING LAND

Humans have destroyed many lemur habitats. Lemurs have fewer places to live. And they can't find food as easily. Many species are **endangered**.

CHAPTER 4

LIFE CYCLE

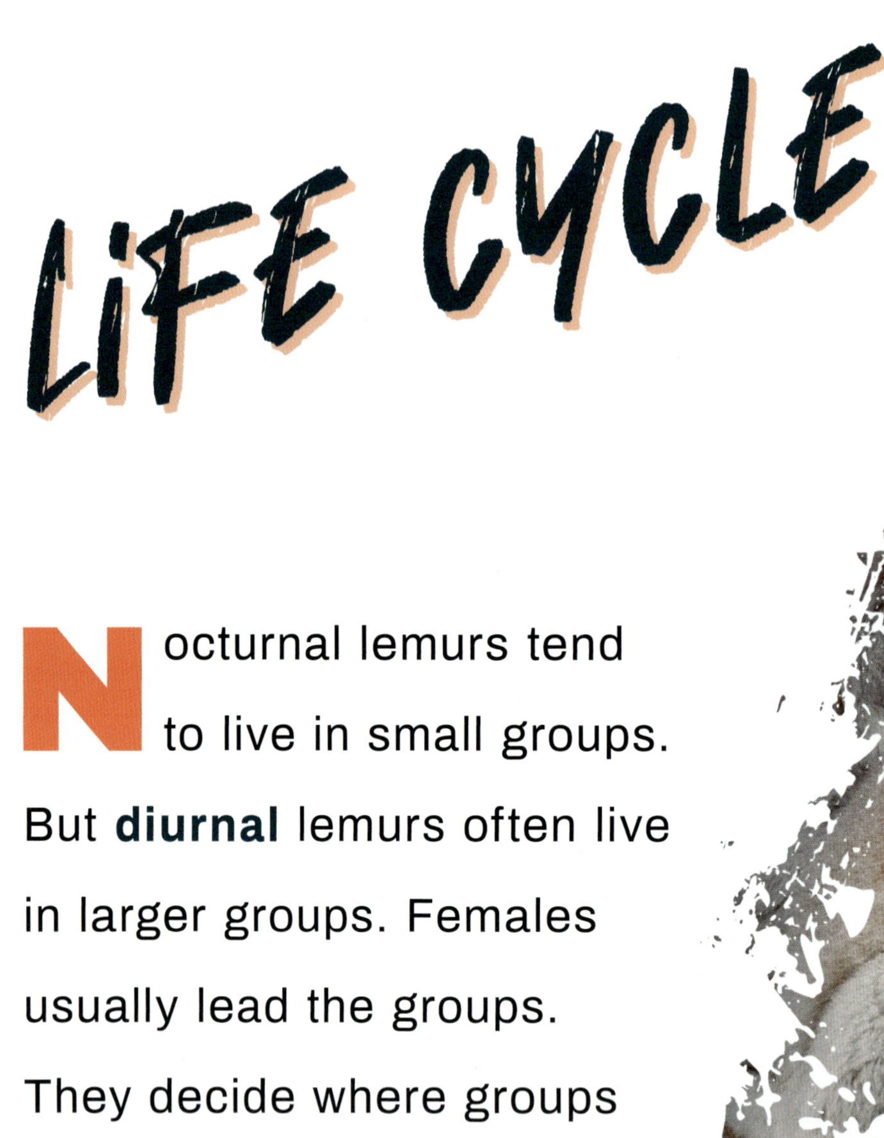

Nocturnal lemurs tend to live in small groups. But **diurnal** lemurs often live in larger groups. Females usually lead the groups. They decide where groups go and what they eat.

Lemurs live in groups called troops. Some troops include dozens of lemurs.

Baby lemurs often cling to their mothers' bodies.

Lemurs have a **mating season**. Females give birth a few months after mating. Some species have one baby at a time. Others may have up to six.

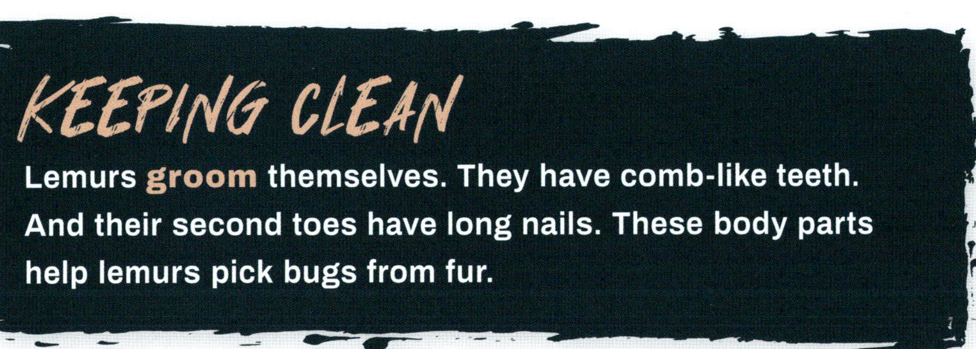

KEEPING CLEAN

Lemurs **groom** themselves. They have comb-like teeth. And their second toes have long nails. These body parts help lemurs pick bugs from fur.

Lemurs may groom one another's fur.

At first, babies stay very close to their mothers. After a few months, they can move and find food on their own. By about 1.5 years old, they are fully grown.

Baby lemurs drink their mothers' milk at first.

COMPREHENSION QUESTIONS

Write your answers on a separate piece of paper.

1. Write a few sentences describing the places where lemurs live.

2. What fact about lemurs do you find most interesting? Why?

3. How long do the largest lemurs grow?

- **A.** 5 inches (12.7 cm)
- **B.** 28 inches (71 cm)
- **C.** 50 inches (127 cm)

4. How could warning noises help lemurs avoid danger?

- **A.** Lemurs could hear the noises and have time to run away.
- **B.** Lemurs could move toward danger when they hear the noises.
- **C.** Lemurs could use the noises to find food.

5. What does **alert** mean in this book?

They bark, grunt, and yell. Some noises are warnings. Lemurs may ***alert*** *one another of danger.*

- **A.** to fall asleep high in a tree
- **B.** to let someone know something is happening
- **C.** to stay quiet for a long time

6. What does **diets** mean in this book?

Different lemur species have different ***diets****. Some lemurs mainly eat plants.*

- **A.** animals' home areas
- **B.** animals' life cycles
- **C.** animals' usual food

Answer key on page 32.

GLOSSARY

diurnal

Awake and active during the day.

endangered

In danger of dying out forever.

groom

To clean or care for an animal's fur.

habitats

The places where animals usually live.

mating season

The time of year when animals form pairs and come together to have babies.

primates

Animals in a group that includes apes and monkeys.

species

Groups of animals or plants that are similar and can breed with one another.

territory

An area that an animal or group of animals lives in and defends.

BOOKS

Becker, Trudy. *Aye-Ayes*. Apex Editions, 2025.

Doeden, Matt. *Travel to Madagascar.* Lerner Publications, 2024.

Jaycox, Jaclyn. *Ring-Tailed Lemur Princesses: Rulers of the Troop*. Capstone Publishing, 2023.

ONLINE RESOURCES

Visit **www.apexeditions.com** to find links and resources related to this title.

ABOUT THE AUTHOR

Trudy Becker lives in Minneapolis, Minnesota. Her grandpa called her a lemur when she was a baby.

INDEX

ANSWER KEY:

1. Answers will vary; 2. Answers will vary; 3. B; 4. A; 5. B; 6. C